The **Ultimate** Beginner's Guide To PPC: Start Using Google Ads Like A Pro [2024]

Sophie Fell

Head of Paid Media at Two Trees PPC

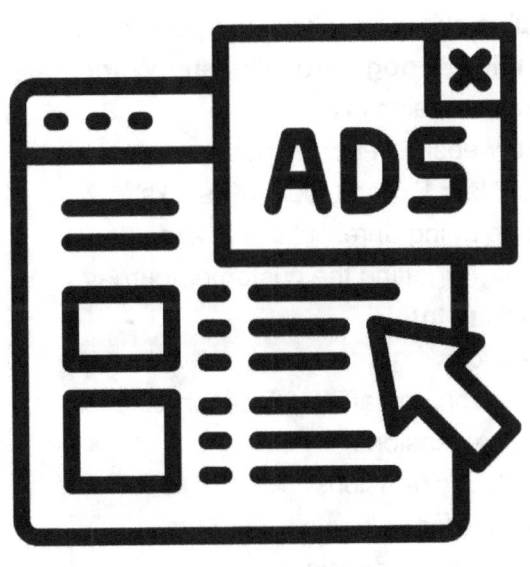

Introductions

Welcome!

My name is Sophie Fell and I'm the Head of Paid Media at Two Trees PPC. Over the last 8+ years of experience in all things PPC, I've strategized, created, optimized and managed more than 300 Google Ads accounts — responsible for everything from strategy, planning and research to execution and optimization.

I've worked with major UK brands such as Madame Tussauds, The London Eye, LEGO, Indeed, FILA, Juicy Couture and Hotel Chocolat. And now, you!

I love helping businesses of all shapes and sizes get to grips with their Google Ads and PPC efforts! If you're someone who wants to learn more about how to create campaigns and ads that actually work, you're in the right hands.

This guide is split into several sections for super-simple navigation, or you can read it from beginning to end. I hope you find it useful! Now, let's begin...

Chapter One: What Is PPC?

The term is most often used synonymously with Google Ads (or, far less often, Microsoft Ads).

PPC (pay-per-click) allows businesses to obtain targeted traffic from search engines, social media or display partners to their website. PPC is considered a more 'inbound' or 'pull' form of digital marketing, as you're capturing demand as they are actively searching for what you offer. And, as a business, you'll only pay when your ads are clicked, boosting your brand awareness in the process!

This method of digital marketing is brilliant for companies who want to:

1. Increase their brand awareness and visibility
2. Generate overnight traffic from their target audience
3. Create demand for their products and services

While these three are all positives, you'll notice that PPC marketing does not guarantee sales or other conversions, it simply drives (interested!) traffic to your website.

With 6.9 billion Google searches and 900 million Microsoft searches per day, it's easy to wonder — how on earth do search engines decide what the best results are for every search query? This is where the auction process comes in.

1.1. The auction process

Google explains it as, "[t]he process that happens with each Google search to decide which ads will appear for that specific search and in which order those ads will show on the page (or whether or not any ads will show at all). Each time an ad is eligible to appear for a search, it goes through the ad auction".

Each platform has its own considerations based on the maximum bid, quality score, ad extensions, relevance and ad rank. Think of the auction process similar to an eBay auction, with multiple businesses placing bids, increasing £/$0.01 a time, to show their ad in front of each customer when they search.

If you're using the Manual CPC (cost-per-click) or Maximize Clicks bidding strategies, you can set the maximum you're willing to pay per click either at the ad group or individual keyword levels. All other automated bid strategies will work within your total daily budget set to deliver results, whether that's clicks, visibility or sales. Don't worry! We'll cover this more throughout this guide.

Chapter Two: Get To Know Your Google Ads Account

Create your account through ads.google.com and click Start Now. Fill in your basic business and billing information, and that's it!

Secret extra tip: When creating a brand new ads account, Google usually encourages you to create a 'SMART' campaign, where you create a campaign by adding your URL, creating an ad, applying a budget, and away you go! This sounds (and is) simple, but it gives you virtually no control over your keywords and only gives you the option to create one version of ad copy. Avoid this and click 'Switch To Expert Mode' if the option is available.

Google Ads has a very structured hierarchy to follow:

Account > Campaign > Ad Group > Ads > Keywords

Let's explore some of these…

2.1. Campaigns

A set of ad groups organized into relevant categories. For example, as an eCommerce store, you may have a 'jackets' campaign, with separate ad groups within it for women's jackets and men's jackets.

There are several forms of campaigns within Google Ads. The best place to start when choosing a campaign type is by goal setting. Figure out the goals that you want your Google Ads to achieve. Whether that's:

- Brand awareness
- More traffic
- More impressions
- Conversions
- Local store visits and shop footfall
- App downloads and/or engagements

Remember too that conversions aren't just sales — conversions are the desired action that you want visitors to complete while on your website. A conversion could be:

- Purchases
- Video views
- Phone calls
- Lead form submissions
- Product downloads
- App downloads
- Newsletter subscriptions
- In-person store visits

Based on your advertising goals, you can choose from Search, Display, Performance Max, Shopping, Video, App, Smart, Local or Discovery campaigns! To begin with, I'd always suggest selecting search — the majority of this guide is exclusively about search ads.

Secret extra tip: When creating a brand new ads account, Google usually encourages you to create a 'SMART' campaign, where you create a campaign by adding your URL, create an ad, apply a budget, and away you go! This sounds (and is) simple, but it gives you virtually no control over your keywords and only gives you the option to create one version of ad copy. We wouldn't recommend using this; the tips below will make your ads much more effective.

2.1.1. Campaign types

2.1.1.1. App campaigns

Made for businesses with apps. Promote app installs, app engagements and app sign-ups across the Google Network: Search, Display, Play and YouTube from one campaign.

2.1.1.2. Display campaigns

Display campaigns are image-based ads that appear across the Google Network. They are most commonly used for creating brand awareness, retargeting and dynamic retargeting purposes.

2.1.1.3. Local campaigns

Local campaigns are used for local shops, physical events and venues. They appear across Google Search, Maps, Display and YouTube to encourage local shop visits as well as providing directions and opening hours of your business.

2.1.1.4. Performance Max campaigns

Performance Max campaigns are a relatively new form of campaign type that allow you to access all of Google's inventory within a single campaign. They can be used for a wide range of conversion types and lean heavily on AI and automation to create the most effective ad for each individual search query.

2.1.1.5. Search campaigns

Search campaigns show ads on the Google SERP and are text-based. However, some ads also now include imagery. These can be used for all stages of the marketing funnel, but are at their most effective when used for mid and lower-funnel campaigns.

2.1.1.6. Shopping campaigns

Shopping campaigns are ideal for eCommerce brands and businesses that sell products with inventory. These ads often appear at the top of the SERP as well as on the Google Shopping tab, highlighting products, product descriptions, imagery and pricing to encourage online sales.

2.1.1.7. SMART campaigns

SMART campaigns are super-simple ads to create where the advertiser only needs to specify business goals, budget, location and final URL. Google's machine-learning algorithm creates keywords and ad copy as well as auto-optimizing the campaign.

In Google UKI's own words, *"The staff of a fish and chip shop in Derby, for example, may be too busy serving food during their shifts to dedicate any time to optimizing the bids on each of their Google Ads. With Smart campaigns, they no longer need to manage this process manually. Google's technology will identify terms like "haddock" and "battered sausage" as relevant to the business and automatically show ads to nearby potential customers searching for those terms"*.

2.1.1.7. Video campaigns

Video campaigns can be used for all stages of the marketing funnel: from awareness to lead generation. These campaigns will appear across YouTube and, where applicable, third-party video websites.

2.2. Ad groups

An ad group is a group of adverts and keywords that share a theme, with similar target audiences. A fashion eCommerce store would have ad groups for each of its products or product categories. As above, women's jackets and men's jackets would be part of two different ad groups, as they have two distinct (but similar) audiences. However, both ad groups would appear under the same campaign for Jackets.

2.3 Ads

An ad (or advertisement) is your means of communication with the customer. They type in a search term and your ad should appear! Ideally, your ad will contain useful information about your product, service, business and USPs (unique selling points). This should encourage the customer to visit your website to learn more.

2.3.1. Call-only ads

These ads encourage phone calls rather than visits to your website. This form of ad uses two 30-character headlines, your business name, two 90-character descriptions and your business phone number.

2.3.2. Dynamic search ads (DSAs)

These types of ads use ad copy that's dynamically generated based on the content of your website and automatically sends users to the best landing page on your website to match their search query. With this form of ad, you only need to enter two 90-character descriptions; Google does the rest for you.

2.3.3. Expanded text ads

Expanded text ads use three static headlines (30 characters) and two static descriptions (90 characters). Since June 2022, editing current expanded text ads and creating new ones is no longer allowed — however, expanded text ads created before this point can still run. Instead, Google is encouraging businesses to use Responsive Search Ads.

2.3.4. Responsive search ads (RSAs)

By adding up to 15 options for headline descriptions (30 characters) and four options for descriptions (90 characters), Google automatically tests and optimizes the best-performing combinations of ad copy in each auction. This improves the CTR (click-through rate) of your ads by making them super-relevant to each search query.

Chapter Three: Keywords

Within each of your ad groups, you may use one or several keywords to tell search engines which search terms you want your ads to appear for.

I've put together a whistle-stop tour of the three forms of keyword match types below in order from least restrictive and most broad, to most restrictive and least broad.

3.1. Broad match keywords

The first of the three and the default keyword match type.

Example: Women's red jacket

A broad match keyword will trigger the appearance of your ad if someone types in a search term related to either:

- One of the words used (jacket store near me)
- Related keywords to your entire keyword/keyphrase (women's jacket)
- The keywords in any order (red women's jacket)
- Misspellings (red jakit)

Broad match keywords deliver a lot of impressions and, subsequently, clicks — but may deliver lower quality traffic due to 'loose' matching. You'll need to keep a close eye on the Search Terms Report and add negative keywords to keep your search terms relevant.

Sidenote: you may have heard of 'Broad Match Modifier' as a form of keyword match type. Example: +womens +red +jacket. This is no longer supported by either Google or Microsoft Ads and cannot be created. If you have broad match modifier keywords on your live ad groups, they'll be treated as phrase match keywords instead.

3.2. Phrase match keywords

The second of the three keyword match types. Middle-of-the-road in terms of reach and restrictive nature.

Example: "women's red jacket"

A phrase match keyword will trigger the appearance of your ad if someone types in:

- The phrase as it is (women's red jacket)
- The phrase with words on either side (buy women's red jacket, women's red jacket online)

- Re-ordered ONLY if the intent is the same (red women's jacket)

Phrase match keywords are known as moderate matching. They're likely to deliver higher-quality traffic and more relevant traffic to your website. These users will have more intent behind their searches than if they matched with broad match keywords.

3.3. Exact match keywords

The last of the three keyword match types. The most restrictive in nature and low reach, but very accurate.

Example: [women's red jacket]

An exact match keyword will trigger the appearance of your ad if someone types in:

- The keyword exactly as it is with nothing before or after (womens red jacket)
- Very close variants such as misspellings, punctuations, synonyms, minor variations and reordered words (womens red jackets, womens red jacket)
- Search terms with the same meaning as your keyword (ladies crimson coat)

Exact match keywords are known as tight matching. You're likely to receive fewer impressions and clicks, but those that do click will be very high in intent and pre-qualified website visitors. Generally speaking, CTR for exact match keywords is much higher than phrase match or keyword match types.

Keyword considerations:

- Google and Microsoft are currently pushing users to 'upgrade' their keywords to broad match — be careful with this and test a small sub-section of keywords before blindly changing all keyword match types to broad.
- "Adding very similar keywords, such as 'red car' and 'car red' isn't recommended, as only one keyword would match both searches. However, doing so won't affect your costs or performance in any way" — Google Support
- Keep in mind the goals of your advertising and your audience — if you're looking to increase your brand reach and awareness, broad match keywords are great. If you need more defined campaigns with want to drive conversions, exact match keywords are better to reach higher-intent audiences
- Check Google's Keyword Planner (or your choice of keyword research tool) for search volumes and CPCs before starting. This ensures that there's sufficient demand for your terms, especially if you're only using exact match keywords.

Chapter Four: How To Optimize Your Campaigns

Even the best of us rarely get Google Ads right the first time. And, often, predictions made (by Google themselves) don't match up with reality — sometimes for the better, sometimes for worse. The main thing about being a Google Ad wizard is a willingness to learn and make changes based on the data.

Here are some of the most common things I check when auditing or optimizing a Google Ads account...

4.1. Location, location, location

This is a super easy *mistake* (or, non-mistake because Google deliberately hides this setting) to make that can quickly drain a budget while delivering absolutely no relevant results. The default in the UK for ads is to target the whole of the United Kingdom, similarly to the United States. And, in some cases, that's the most appropriate choice if you have a huge budget and want to make a national splash.

However, for small businesses and service providers, niching down to your local area ensures that not only are you maximizing your available budget but also that your ads aren't wasted on people outside of your target audience or service area.

The other *mistake* is that, by default, your ads will show to people *interested* in the area in which your ads are targeting. For example, someone might consider visiting Stonehenge during their visit from any other country in the world. This will then show them ads for other businesses, events or service providers in the Stonehenge area, regardless of relevancy or proximity to where they actually are.

Target ⑦

○ People in, or who show interest in, your targeted locations (recommended)

◉ People in or regularly in your targeted locations

○ People searching for your targeted locations

Transform your ad performance almost instantaneously by switching this over via your campaign settings — make sure your ads only show to those living in your area of choice, not those who are interested in it.

4.2. The magic 3% rule

For Search campaigns and ad groups, it's important to aim for a 3% CTR as a minimum. If you're not achieving this yet — and your campaigns have been running for several weeks or months by now — this is a must-fix. Common reasons for this covered below.

CTR is the number of clicks that your ad receives divided by the number of times your ad is shown: clicks ÷ impressions = CTR. For example, if your ad was viewed 100 times (impressions) and was clicked 5 times, your CTR would be 5%.

CTR is a key indicator of the relevancy of your keywords, ad copy and landing page content. If your CTR is low, your Quality Score will be low and you'll find it hard to outbid your competition to appear in the SERP.

For example, a small business sells homemade tapestry. If the headlines and descriptions on the ads themselves don't allude to and include tapestry-related keywords as part of the content, the ads are unlikely to be clicked by the prospective customer. Demonstrating relevance between what the user is looking for (using their search terms) and your ad copy is critical.

A quick overview can be obtained by looking at your Campaign Overview and starting with the campaign with the lowest CTR. Use 3% as a benchmark: the lower the number, the bigger the priority to adjust. Check poorly-performing keywords, pause weak ad copy and review Google's ad copy suggestions if there are any — just don't 'auto-apply' any suggestions without checking first!

4.3. Double-check your keyword performance

The next step is to check your keywords. Click on your campaign, then ad groups, select an ad group and view keywords. Within the list, look out for these two keyword statuses:

- 'Below first-page bid'
- 'Below the top of page bid'

If you're using Manual CPC as a bidding strategy, these keywords don't have enough budget behind them to get your ads to the first page or the top of the first page of search results. If you're comfortable, increase the keyword bids to the suggested amount so the keyword will trigger ads more often.

Similarly, it's key to look for limited or ineligible keyword statuses — these are usually due to low search volumes. First, check the spelling of your keyword, this is a common cause of this. If the spelling is right, consider making the keyword less niche so it'll appear more regularly.

Review your keyword performance over the last period: one week, one month, a quarter or your choice of timeframe. This can be done using the calendar in the top-right of the Google Ads interface and setting start and end dates manually, or by selecting a pre-defined time frame and clicking Save. Some keywords may be made eligible to appear but not appear as often as they should, whereas others may receive 0 impressions. If that's the case, make changes such as altering the keyword text or the keyword match type if it's too restrictive.

Chapter Five: When Google Ads Doesn't Work

One of the reasons why PPC (pay-per-click) marketing is so successful and highly adopted is because you only pay when you get results — clicks. At a very basic level, in theory, what you put in in terms of budget, you get out in the form of website traffic. However, it's not all rainbows, unicorns and pink fluffy clouds... let's explore some situations when PPC won't help you generate sales.

5.1. Your campaign is bad

One of the most obvious reasons for a lack of results from PPC: a terrible campaign.

I'll keep this short. If your campaign(s) doesn't have good landing pages, excellent ad strength RSAs (Responsive Search Ads), a mixture of relevant phrase match and exact match keywords with great quality scores and a relevant set of negative keywords in place, start here.

When auditing or optimizing Google Ads campaigns, I look for:

- 15–30 relevant keywords per ad group
- Relevant location targeting (those *in* your target area, not just interested in)
- A landing page that includes various keywords from the ad group
- At least one RSA with an ad strength of Good/Excellent
- A 3–6% CTR on the ad group as a whole
- At least two forms of ad extensions such as sitelinks, callouts and structured snippets
- Keywords with quality scores of 6/10+
- Some negative keywords applied

If your ad groups and campaigns already have the above list as well as working conversion tracking in place, move on to the next steps. If not, optimize your campaigns accordingly until the checklist above is complete.

5.2. Your website performs poorly

Unfortunately, you could create the most targeted and well-optimized campaign possible and still be left with a lack of conversions. Let's take a look at why this is and how to fix it...

If you know your campaigns are good, the next place to look is your website analytics. Even if your campaigns are in the best possible place, the impact of a weak website cannot be underestimated. Sending targeted traffic to a website that doesn't work, loads slowly or has a poor mobile experience won't do your business (or its reputation) any favors.

Not only does a technically poor website affect your Ad Rank — an important Google Ads bidding factor —, but it will also affect your Search Engine Optimisation (SEO) efforts. Use a free tool such as Google PageSpeed Insights to analyze the experience of your website on desktop and mobile; this tool will also give you specifics on what needs updating and improving.

Don't forget that Google ranks and indexes websites based on the mobile experience first, so don't ignore your total website experience on smaller devices.

5.3. Your User Experience (UX) sucks

Aligned with point two is point three: a poor user experience. It's one thing if your 'Technical SEO' is poor, but on-page UX is another factor to consider when understanding a lack of conversions or sales from PPC traffic. Poor UX leads to abandoned checkouts, high bounce rates and unhappy web visitors.

Here are some common causes of a bad UX:

- Blurry, pixelated, low-quality images or generic stock imagery
- Unclear or broken website navigation
- Hidden/difficult to view/non-clickable CTAs
- An elongated checkout/conversion process
- A lack of relevant information or out-of-date content
- Frequent pop-ups — including invasive/persistent live chat
- Lack of search functionality
- Text-heavy web pages (with multiple large blocks of text)

Beyond these factors, demonstrating expertise, authority and trust (E-A-T) is another key to encouraging a visitor to convert. Put simply, if customers can't find the trust indicators they expect to verify the credibility of your brand and its products or services, they won't buy and may not ever return to your website. There are very few second chances in online brand reputation.

Some good ways to demonstrate credibility on your website include:

- Customer feedback such as reviews, testimonials and case studies
- A secure HTTPS domain and SSL certificate
- A physical address and contact information
- Links to your social media channels
- Client showcases
- Links to featured PR and press

- Awards and nominations

5.4. You're being unrealistic with expectations

2022 research from Wordstream has shown that the average conversion rate on Google Ads varies considerably between industries from 2% for apparel/fashion, jewelry and furniture to 15% for animals, pets, doctors, physicians and surgeons.

So, even if you're creating ads for an industry with a typically high conversion rate, 85% of the time, your Search ads won't convert. It's important to be reasonable about this. Generally speaking, a conversion rate between 2-3% on Search is good to aim for — a 97-98% **non-conversion rate**.

5.5. You're forgetting the customer journey

Finally, be realistic about the customer journey and the sales funnel. Unless your keywords are "I want to buy [brand's] [product] online right now" (unlikely), user search intent and context are regularly up for debate.

It's rare that a customer will purchase after their first and only exposure to a brand and its products; a search query and subsequent click could come from any stage in the user's buying journey. Although, generic product searches tend to be in the upper part of the sales funnel, with branded searches further down it.

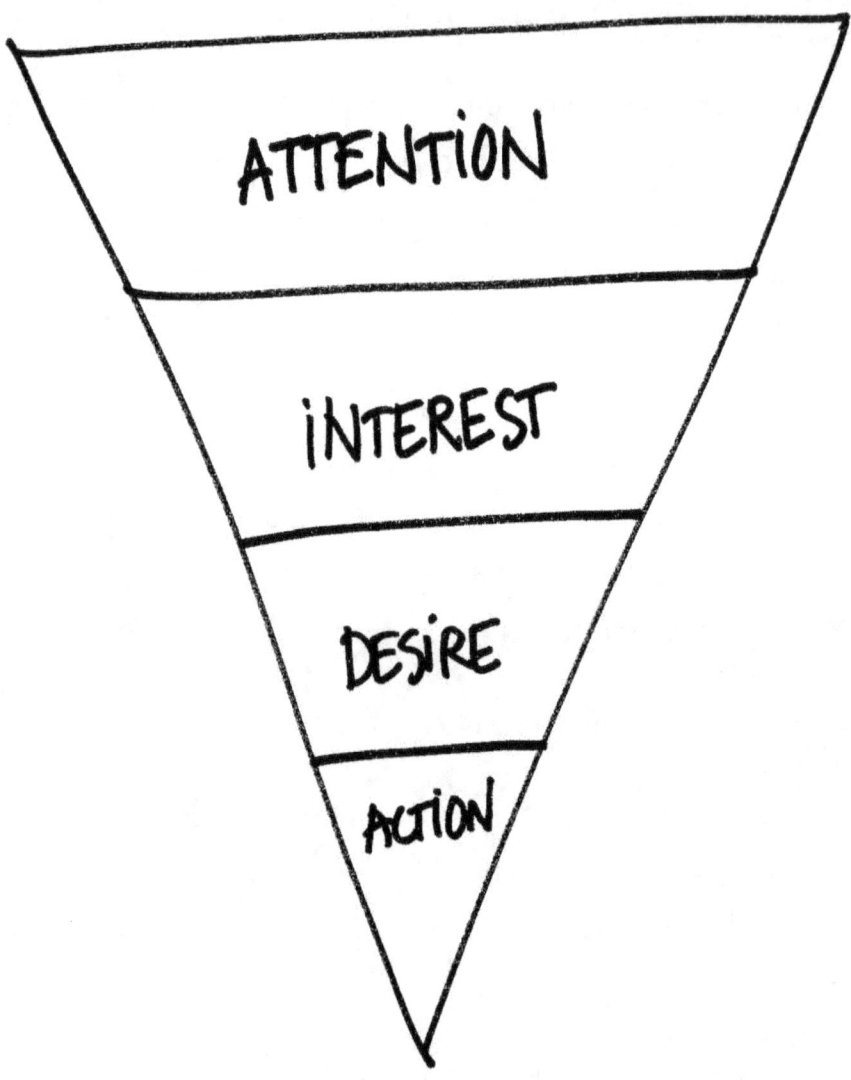

(Source: drivinmissdaisy)

The key is to remember that clicks don't often mean that a customer is ready to buy. With online businesses more numerous and competitive than ever before, online shoppers are increasingly relying on trust signals such as customer reviews and personal recommendations to inform their purchasing decisions.

Or, maybe they're just researching when they land on your website — that's okay too. A robust retargeting strategy can support you here to keep prospective customers within your funnel. Use programmatic advertising and/or social media ads to encourage your customers to return to your website to check out — this is a good place for discount codes and incentives! Just don't expect a 10%, 25% or even 50% conversion rate. Today, the user journey contains more touchpoints than ever before; users may browse a website multiple times before converting.

Chapter Six: Bonus Intel

AKA important things to know that I couldn't squeeze in elsewhere!

6.1. Ad extensions

Ad extensions appear underneath the ad itself on the SERP (search engine results page) to add more information to the person who sees the ad. This may include location information, phone numbers, USPs or a list of services offered.

Ad extensions are great because they:

- Take up more space on the SERP
- Don't cost any extra when clicked
- Boost your ad rank, making it more likely that your ad will appear
- Increase your CTR.

There are plenty of ad extensions to choose from and multiple forms of ad extension can appear at the same time. Let's take a quick tour of which types of ad extensions are available and when to use them.

6.1.1. Location and affiliate location extensions

Perfect for businesses with a physical location who sell products in their stores or via affiliate stores. These ad extensions are made up of just your business name (or affiliate business name) and address. When they appear via Google, a pin will also appear showing the user how far (at the time of search) they are from your business or nearest business location or will direct users to retail stores near them that sell your products or provide your service(s).

- Business name
- Address

Adding a location extension to your Google Ads campaign is one of the best ways possible for businesses with one, or several, locations to increase visits and footfall. And, when a local customer searches for '[your product or service] near me', your ads will appear. Simply link your Google My Business account to your Google Ads account to start the process.

Secret extra tip: If you don't already have a GMB account, create one immediately! There are so many perks including a free listing on Google Maps to help customers find you, as well as sharing directions, accessibility information, photos and contact details online. It's a big win for local SEO, so I implore you to make one as soon as you possibly can. In fact, do it now. And then come back and read the rest of this book.

Affiliate location extensions are used in a similar way, but direct users to retail stores near them that sell your products or provide your services.

6.1.2. Call extensions

Perfect for businesses with inbound sales or leads predominantly from phone calls. This one is simple. Simply create a call extension, add your business phone number to it and Google will display your phone number attached to your ad if they believe that doing so is likely to result in a conversion. In an ideal world, this phone number would be used exclusively for inbound product enquiries rather than customer service or brand searches for tracking purposes!

Call extensions can be tracked and measured as Google Ads conversions. You can also use a different (dynamic and trackable) number if you want to track calls from call extensions — these are auto-created and tracked by Google.

6.1.3. Callout extensions

Perfect for all businesses. Callout extensions are made up of several individual callouts with a 25-character limit. Not to be confused with call extensions!

Sometimes, 30-character headlines and 90-character descriptions aren't enough. Callout ad extensions give you the opportunity to highlight any useful features or benefits of your product or service. These can be applied at the ad group level to make them unique to each of your products/services.

Alternatively, create and apply callout extensions at the campaign level to showcase the best bits of your brand: Free Next Day Delivery, 20 Years Of Experience, Award-Winning Team, Experts In [Industry] etc. Up to 10 callouts can appear at once — so don't be afraid to add plenty for the algorithm to choose from.

6.1.4. Structured snippets

Perfect for all businesses. Structured snippet extensions are made up of a predefined header and 25-character headlines.

Structured snippets are similar to callout extensions, with one critical difference: they are pre-defined. So, instead of (read: as well as...) showing off your features, perks and USPs with callouts, sitelinks allow you to showcase the most relevant options, choices and selections to your business. The predefined headers include the following:

- Amenities
- Brands
- Courses
- Degree programs
- Destinations
- Featured hotels
- Insurance cover
- Models
- Areas
- Service catalog
- Shows
- Styles
- Types

As each of your ad groups will be themed, use structured snippets to expand on your offering.

Brands: Nike, Adidas, EA Sports, New Balance
Service catalog: Wheel Alignment, Oil Changes, Winter Car Check, Tire Pressure
Areas: Manhattan, Brooklyn, Queens, Times Square.

Secret extra tip: While you're not limited to adding four structured snippets, only four will appear at a time in the SERP, and Google will select which four. Similarly, you can create multiple versions and, again, apply them at different levels of your account, but only one set of structured snippets will appear at a time.

6.1.5. Lead form extensions

Perfect for B2B and lead-generating businesses. Lead form extensions are an effective way of gathering customer data and increasing conversion rates without incurring any additional cost.

Lead forms are made up of:

- A 30-character headline
- Your business name

- A 200-character description
- Questions (pre-defined for contact information and work information by Google)
- Qualifying questions (pre-defined from a large list sorted by industry)
- Your business' privacy policy URL
- A background image
- From submission message with CTA
- Call-to-action button and a 30-character description

Unfortunately, lead form extensions aren't available to everyone. Google has created some specific guidance on this to understand whether or not your account is eligible. Use lead form extensions to instantly gather data from the SERP, rather than converting prospects from your website. You can either download the available data from Google Ads into a CSV file, or you can link Google Ads to your CRM to add live data as it comes in.

6.1.6. Price extensions

Perfect for eCommerce and service-led online businesses. Price extensions work well for online businesses that sell D2C. Whether product prices are 'From...' or an exact figure, this form of ad extension will not only display the prices for your products and services, but will allow customers to directly access the product they're interested in (at the right price point) from the SERP. This gives the competitive edge, particularly for businesses that are priced competitively.

Price extensions are made up of:

- Language, currency, type and price qualifier (such as from, up to and average)
- 25-character headline
- Product or service value (including units: no unit, per hour, per day, per week, per month, per year or per night)
- 25-character description
- Final URL and choice of mobile URL

The other big benefit is screening and pre-qualifying your audience — they are likely only to click on the ad if that particular product or service is within their budget: the perfect conversion rate booster!

6.1.7. Promotion extensions

Perfect for: eCommerce businesses. While eCommerce businesses are no stranger to the annual calendar of key shopping dates, promotion extensions provide a much-needed boost to ad campaigns. Not only are they ideal for time-sensitive events such as Mother's Day or Valentine's Day, but they can also be used for non-specific periods such as winter or end-of-season sales.

Promotion extensions are made up of:

- A predefined occasion from a list (i.e. Back to school, Black Friday, Cyber Monday, Eid al-Adha, etc.)
- Language and currency
- Promotion type (monetary discount, percent discount, 'up to' monetary discount or 'up to' percent discount)
- Item
- Final URL
- Promotion details (such as on orders over or a promo code)
- Start and end date

The flexibility of promotion extensions is a key feature. They are simple to edit and can be scheduled to start and stop in advance.

6.1.8. Sitelink extensions

Perfect for businesses with a large website or wide range of products or services. You can use sitelink extensions to tailor the customer journey from the SERP — in a similar way to price extensions. Underneath your ad, sitelink extensions will appear to direct users to other web pages that may interest them. This could be customer testimonials and reviews, a portfolio, a product list, contact information etc.

Sitelinks extensions are made up of:

- 25-character headline text
- Two 35-character description lines
- Final URL

Sitelink extensions that use both 35-character description lines are one of the best ways to take up more search engine real estate beneath your ad.

6.1.9. App extensions

Perfect for: Businesses with apps! If one of your business goals or key metrics is to encourage app downloads or interactions, app extensions provide an effective and trackable way of doing so. And, if you add both Android and iOS app extensions, Google will automatically detect which device the user is browsing from and only provide them with the relevant link to them. This saves pesky landing pages with multiple download links.

App extensions are made up of:

- An app platform (Android or iOS, or create separate ad extensions for both platforms if available on both)
- The app name
- A 'Download Now' automated CTA.

"Okay, you've convinced me... How do I add an ad extension?"

- Log into your Google Ads account
- On the left-hand menu, click 'Ads & extensions'
- This menu will then open to show 'Ads' and 'Extensions' separately. Click 'Extensions'
- Click the blue + sign on the page and select which form of ad extension to apply

- At the top, it will say 'Add to' — select Account, Campaign or Ad group
- Fill in the necessary information and click the blue 'Save' button.

It's as easy as that!

6.2 Negative keywords

While a keyword specifies when to show certain ads based on the user's search term, a negative keyword does exactly the opposite by telling the search engine *not* to show your ads when certain keywords are used.

A super-simple example of this is a Google search for 'trainers'. In American English we'd commonly use **'sneakers'**, but to clarify this point - let's imagine you are appealing to the international English language community. If your eCommerce or brick-and-mortar store sells men's trainers, you might be tempted to use 'trainers' as a broad match keyword. But, it's important to consider all the other potential homonyms that the user might be referring to with their search query.

- Personal trainer
- Cross trainer

- Virtual trainer
- Dog trainer
- Animal trainer

There are also other services that may apply that are relevant to 'shoe' trainers, but aren't what your store sells in this scenario.

- Kids trainers
- Women's trainers
- Trainer repair
- How to clean trainers
- Shoelaces for trainers
- Personalized trainers
- Hiking trainers
- Design your own trainers

There are two separate ways to get around this — I recommend using them in conjunction with each other.

1. Stay away from broad match keywords and generic terms such as 'trainer' and be more specific with your keywords. Use phrase match keywords ("phrase match") or exact match ([exact match]) keywords to niche this down. "Men's trainers", "Men's running trainers" and "Men's black trainers" are good examples of what to do here without being too restrictive.

2. Use negative keywords. As well as making your keywords more specific using keyword match types, add negative keywords to reduce irrelevant terms. You can add negative keywords as broad match, phrase match or exact match. I usually add them as broad match for single words such as 'cross' or 'jobs' and phrase match for phrases such as "shoe repair" — in the latter, you don't necessarily want to add 'shoe' as a negative keyword, but the phrase as a whole.

You may also want to be more specific about the colors, brands and types of men's trainers that are available. Negative keywords can be used here to do this. Maybe your shoes aren't suitable for men with wide feet or for those who want velcro straps. Use 'wide', "wide feet" or 'velcro' to avoid these searches.

"Do I need to use negative keywords?" You say. "Definitely!!" I reply.

If your keywords are too generic and subject to tens of thousands of impressions daily, you'll end up with a lot of wasted impressions to uninterested customers as well as wasted clicks, which will quickly eat up your budget.

While Google's ranking factors are still *somewhat* of a secret, what we do know is that your Quality Score is a critical component. Your Quality Score is informed, at least in part, by your historic CTR and the anticipated CTR at each auction.

If your ads have thousands of impressions and very few clicks or a high bounce rate when people do click them, Google will think your content is irrelevant to the search query and the user. Your CTR will be low as a result of this and your Google Ads will suffer as a whole — leading to a higher CPC (cost-per-click) to outbid the competition for relevant clicks and an ongoing struggle to outbid the competition. Basically, please add negatives so as not to completely destroy your Google Ads.

6.2.1. Where can I use negative keywords?

You can apply negative keywords at either the campaign level or ad group level. Adding them at the campaign level will exclude those keywords from all ad groups within that particular campaign.

At the ad group level, you can use negative keywords to avoid crossover between ad groups. For example, if your ad groups apply to different locations (such as California and London) and use the same keywords, consider adding 'California' and 'United States' as negative keywords to the London ad group, and add 'London' and 'England' to the California ad group to keep the two separate; of course, this has to be in conjunction with accurate location targeting.

If you sell several varieties of trainers and your ad groups are separated by color scheme, 'black' or "black trainers" could be applied to an ad group for white trainers only and vice versa. So, use a combination of account-wide (at the campaign level) negative keywords and ad group level negatives for the best results.

6.2.2. How do I find the right negative keywords?

Here are a few tips on where to find the right negative keywords for your business.

Universal negative keyword lists

It's a good idea to make a broad list of negative keywords to apply to all campaigns at the campaign level. This may include universal negatives such as 'free', 'book', 'how to', 'Wikipedia', 'jobs' etc. Webmechanix has an awesome list of 1,500+ negative keywords to use — but double-check them before blindly adding them to your campaigns.

JFGI... Google it!

An easily-accessible source of data is Google — simply Google some of your keywords! Before pressing 'Search' (who am I kidding, no one does that...) before pressing Enter, typing in a search query or phrase will give you suggested searches from Google Suggest autofill. This can give you some initial pointers for irrelevant search terms to avoid.

Once you've searched, you'll end up with a list of results which will include competitor brands, organic searches and the best-performing websites. This is another great source of competitor brands and negative keywords to implement.

Use Keyword Planner

The Google Ads Keyword Planner tool is available to anyone with a Google Ads account. While it's well-known and used for its insights on which keywords you should use, it can also be used to find negative keywords in the same way.

Type in up to 10 search terms and your desired location (such as the United Kingdom, London, United States, New York etc.) and search. You'll end up with a list of potential keywords. While this will give you plenty of inspiration for your ad groups, take note of anything irrelevant that crops up and add it to your negative keyword notes.

Check the Search Terms report

If you already have a Google Ads account running and simply want to reduce the wastage, check your Search Terms report. Note: this is different from your Search Keywords report which shows you the keywords you're currently bidding on. Instead, the Search Terms report shows you the keywords and search terms that have triggered your ads. Check here regularly for irrelevant words or phrases to add to your negative keyword list.

Use your competition

It's important to add competitor brands to your negative keyword list to avoid costly clicks and competing against their enormous budgets!

For example, in super-competitive industries such as trainers, Nike, Adidas, Footlocker, Puma, Converse, Jordans, Vans etc. would be a great place to start. Local competitors should be added too, as this may lead to a high bounce rate if users are searching for another brand and end up on your website.

6.3. Advanced Google Ads Features

Maybe this is the part of the book you've been waiting for. Now you've got the fundamentals sorted, what do the Google Ads professionals do to kick things up a notch?

Relevance is absolutely crucial to creating effective Google Ads. Not only does relevance affect the CTR (click-through rate) of the ads themselves, but it also has an impact on Quality Score which, in turn, affects your ad rank and ability to outbid the competition. Phew!

But how can we ensure that our ads are relevant to each user at scale? Here's where Dynamic Ad Features help: by automatically adjusting your ad copy based on context, machine learning and user search intent.

6.3.1. Match your ad copy to the user's search term

Dynamic Keyword Insertion (DKI) is a feature you can use in your ad headlines or descriptions that will populate the ad copy based on the user's search term.

So, when a user types in 'Men's Ultra Wide Hiking Boots', instead of matching this to a generic 'Men's Boots' headline, your ad will say 'Men's Ultra Wide Hiking Boots'. This boosts the likelihood of that user clicking your ad and, in turn, the CTR of your ad. Remember: 'Expected CTR' is a key element of how Google calculates your Ad Rank.

How? In your headline and/or description from your ad view, add the phrase {Keyword:} with a default phrase to use if the search term can't be used as part of a headline.

For example, if someone is searching for "where can I find men's ultra-wide hiking boots near me?", that keyword is too long due to the 30-character limit on headlines. In this situation, the default headline would be used based on {KeyWord: Men's Black Hiking Boots} — appearing as 'Men's Black Hiking Boots'.

DKI considerations:

1. You can use {Keyword:}, {KeyWord:} or {keyword:} based on the style of your headlines/descriptions. {Keyword:} will deliver sentence case ad copy, whereas {KeyWord:} will use title case — capitalizing each letter, and {keyword:} will be lowercase. Make sure that the style you pick matches the style of your other ad copy to keep it consistent

2. When you begin to type {, Google will give you a drop-down option. Select Keyword and fill the drop-down option's text field with your default keyword. You can also pick whether to use title case, sentence case or lowercase here too

3. Use negative keywords. The last thing you want is rude or entirely irrelevant keywords appearing in your ad copy. In this scenario, it's worth using negative keywords such as 'women', 'women's' or 'kids' to ensure only searches for 'men's boots' trigger your ads

4. You can use the {Keyword:} function in either your headlines or descriptions
5. You can only use this function on search ads.

6.3.2. Use the COUNTDOWN function

The next Dynamic Ad Feature to explore is the countdown function. If you have a key date for tickets to an event, the end of a sale or even a pre-sale, this function will show a live countdown until the event begins. This live countdown will increase urgency and therefore boost CTR.

How? To add a countdown to your ad copy, use either {=COUNTDOWN()} or type in { and choose 'COUNTDOWN' from the drop-down menu. You'll then need to fill in the following data:

Syntax: {=COUNTDOWN("yyyy/MM/dd HH:mm:ss","language",daysBefore)} ⑦

Countdown ends ⑦	7 Apr 2022 ▼
	Start of day ▼ 00:00:00
Countdown starts ⑦	5 day(s) before countdown end date
Time zone ⑦	◯ Account time zone (GMT+01:00) United Kingdom Time
	◉ Ad viewer's time zone
Language ⑦	English (United Kingdom) ▼ Examples: 3 days / 5 hours / 10 mins

APPLY

Countdown considerations:

1. The countdown function doesn't give you the opportunity to add ad copy on either side of the countdown itself. So be sure to add this in the headline field. For example: 'Pre-Sale Live In {COUNTDOWN()}' or 'Quick! Sale Ends In {COUNTDOWN()}'.
2. Remember to check back in on the ads once the event has started/ended and remove this, otherwise you'll be left with very bizarre-looking ads!
3. You can use the {COUNTDOWN{}} function in either your headlines or descriptions
4. You can only use this function on search ads.

6.3.3. IF this, then that...

The third of the Dynamic Ad Features is 'IF'. It can be quite complex to get your head around, but the basics are 'IF this condition is met, DO this'. It's not a must-have by any means — but it's good to use in situations where you'd need to change ad copy per audience or per device. For example, you might want cart abandoners to see a special offer or a discount so they convert, but not for first-time visitors.

Or, you could create audience segments by historical product view and show a different ad if they've previously viewed a certain page on your website rather than just the homepage.

How? Use the formula {=IF(Condition,insert text):default text} or type in { and select from the drop-down.

IF considerations:

1. Make sure your audiences are up-to-date AND that previous visitors are not excluded from seeing your ads
2. You can use the {IF} function in either your headlines or descriptions
3. You can only use this function on search ads.

6.4. Useful tools

These are the must-haves I use day-to-day when running Google Ads accounts.

- Google Analytics
- Google Keyword Planner
- Google PageSpeed Insights
- Google Search Terms Report
- Google Sheets/Microsoft Excel (use the =LEN function when planning ad copy to meet character limits!)
- SEMRush.

Chapter Seven: PPC Jargon Buster

While you've probably got to grips with a lot of the technical jargon by now, here are some other bits of jargon and key phrases to learn.

A/B test

Also known as split testing, A/B testing in this context involves experimenting with different versions of ad creative to see which performs best. You can test landing pages, ad copy, images, audience targeting and more. Once the test is complete, you can continue to run the best-performing ad(s).

Ad rank

Ad rank is simply the position that the ad appears in on the SERP. The first ad on the page would be assigned ad rank 1, the second ad rank 2 and so on.

Ad relevance

The measure of how closely your ad matches what the user is searching for. This can be above average, average or below average.

Attribution model

Attribution models help marketers accurately pinpoint the source or sources of a conversion. Some attribution models such as 'Last click' would give 100% of the credit to the last touchpoint the user engaged with before converting, whereas 'First click' would do the opposite. There are also 'Last non-direct click', 'linear', 'time-decay' and 'position-based' attribution models.

Below first page bid

A keyword status that appears when your maximum bid (or Max. CPC) is not high enough to show your ad on the first page of the SERP.

Below top of page bid

A keyword status that appears when your maximum bid (or Max. CPC) is not high enough to show your ad at the top of the page on the SERP.

Bid

In the auction process, each business offers a maximum bid that they're willing to pay to get their ad in front of that particular customer.

Bidding strategy

Instead of setting manual bids for each keyword, use a bidding strategy (such as maximize clicks, maximize conversions or maximize conversion value) to let Google auto-optimize your ads and bids for your end goal.

Budget

Your daily (and/or monthly) limit of what you're happy to spend on clicks and conversions. (Although Google do say daily costs can vary by up to 20%, but your monthly budget will never exceed what you've set — it'll only vary with the ebbs and flows of traffic each week).

CLTV

Customer lifetime value. The average amount that a customer is 'worth' to a business across the entire length of their relationship.

Multiply your average order total by the average number of purchases made by all customers in a year — this is your customer value. Then, multiply this number by your average retention years. An average order total of $20 multiplied by an average of 3 purchases a year gives you a customer value of $60. Over the span of two years of retention, the CLTV is $120.

Conversion rate

Of the people that clicked your ad, what percentage of those converted? The standard goal is 2–3%, although this is often higher for brand campaigns.

Cost/conv.

Cost per conversion. How much does it cost to convert a customer?

Total ad spend divided by the volume of conversions. $100 spent and 10 conversions gives a cost/conv. of $10.

CPA

Cost per acquisition. How much does it cost to generate a new customer?

Total ad spend divided by the number of new customers acquired. $100 spent and 10 conversions gives a CPA of $10.

CPC

Cost per click. How much does it cost per click?

Total cost divided by the number of clicks. If $10 is spent and 100 clicks are generated, this gives a CPC of $0.10.

CPL

Cost per lead. How much does it cost to generate a lead?

Total cost divided by the volume of leads. If $10 is spent and 1 lead is submitted, this gives a CPL of $10.00.

CPM

Cost per thousand (mille). How much does it cost to gain a thousand impressions?

Total cost divided by the total number of impressions. Then multiply this result by 1,000. If $10 is spent and 1,000 impressions are gained, this gives a CPM of $10.00.

CPV

Cost per view. How much does it cost to generate a single view?

Total cost divided by the total number of views. If $10 is spent and 10,000 views are gained, this gives a CPM of $0.001.

CTR

Click-through rate. Put simply, how many of those who saw an ad clicked on it. A target goal of 3%+ for search campaigns. (3-6% with Responsive Search Ads).

The total number of clicks is divided by the number of impressions. If 10 people clicked on an ad that 100 people saw, the CTR would be 0.10%.

Display URL

Your display URL helps searchers understand where they'll land on your website if they click your ad. This is much more specific and can increase CTR.

Instead of displaying **https://mystore.com/** as your landing page, you can use a Display URL to create

https://mystore.com/womens-jumpers — you have two optional path fields to add information to with 15 characters each. The user will still arrive at the same Final URL — explained below.

ECPC

Enhanced cost per click. Instead of manual bidding where you set a maximum bid for each keyword, ECPC automatically adjusts your bids up or down to meet your goals with your maximum budget in mind.

Final URL

The Final URL is the eventual page on your website that you want users to arrive at — your landing page.

Impressions

Impressions are the total number of times that your content has been displayed. If one user sees the same piece of content fifteen times, that's fifteen impressions. Impressions are counted whether the user clicks on an ad or not.

Impression share (IS)

Impression share is the % of impressions that you received vs the total number of impressions that they could've received.

Keyword planner

A free feature in Google Ads that allows you to plan which keywords to use in your ad groups by giving you data, offering new keyword ideas and giving performance estimates.

Landing page

The page of your website that you want users to 'land' on after clicking your ad. Instead of sending all visitors to the homepage, you'll want to optimize your user journey by sending them to the most relevant page to them based on their search terms.

Long-tail keyword

Unlike a keyword, a long-tail keyword is longer and far more specific. A keyword could be 'men's jacket', whereas a long-tail keyword could be 'blue men's jacket size medium'. Long-tail keywords have lower search volumes as they are niche, but they generally deliver higher-quality traffic.

Low search volume

A keyword status that appears when your keywords have very little (if any) search traffic and are therefore not relevant.

Quality score

This is a measure of how relevant your keywords are to your ads and landing pages. Quality scores are measured from 1–10 (1 being the worst, 10 the best) and are used in the auction process to rank the relevance of your business' keyword vs. that of your competitor.

Reach

Unlike impressions, reach is based on the total number of people who see your content. Whether one particular user sees the same piece of content once or fifteen times, the reach will stay the same.

ROAS

Return on ad spend. Of the total amount spent on ads, how much revenue was generated?

Calculate your ROAS by dividing your total revenue (generated by ads) by the total amount of money you spent on ads. If you spent £/$100 on ads and sold £/$1,000 of product, your ROAS would be 0.1 or 10%.

Search term

The search term is the word or phrase the user types into a search engine.

Search volume

Daily, monthly or yearly search volume is the average number of people who are searching for a particular search query.

SEM

Search engine marketing. The marketing strategy used to promote websites and brands on search engines. SEM is usually about paid advertising whereas...

SEO

... Search engine optimisation focuses on the organic promotion of a website.

SERP

Search engine results page. The results page is seen once a search term has been entered into a search engine. This can be made up of a combination of results including organic, paid, local, maps or shopping ads.

SKAG

Single keyword ad group. Instead of grouping multiple keywords together, SKAGs are ad groups that only contain one keyword. It was once thought that this leads to better control of the account and promotes all keywords fairly. With smart bidding and the automation of Google Ads today, this is no longer necessary and actually contributes to limited results.

Chapter Eight: Final Goodbyes

So, that's everything you'll need to get started with all things Google Ads. If you have any questions, comments or suggestions, please feel free to reach out to Sophie on sophie@twotreesppc.com. And, you can learn more about Two Trees PPC at twotreesppc.com.

Thanks for reading!

www.ingramcontent.com/pod-product-compliance
Lightning Source LLC
Chambersburg PA
CBHW070818290526
45795CB00002B/752